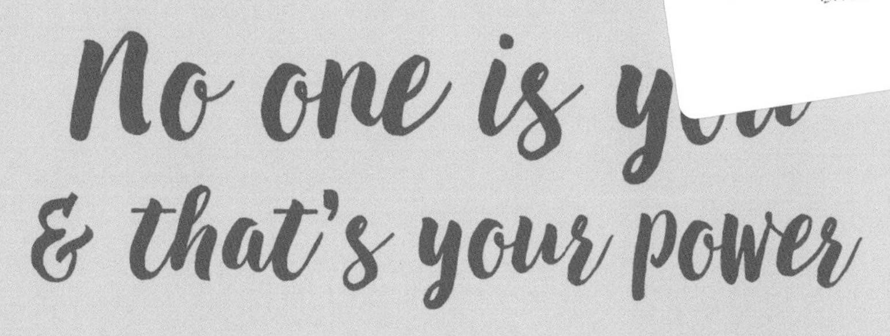

There is no one like you on the planet! You are one of a kind and that needs to be celebrated with lashings of self-love!

Use this guided journal to write down things about yourself. Keep track of your favorite movies, books, hopes and dreams, weirdest things you've ever done, and more. Delve a little deeper to learn about who you are and who you are becoming. Positive quotes and encouragement are sprinkled throughout the pages to keep you company along the way.

When you need to chill there's some coloring pages to express your creativity as well as spaces to doodle and jot down your thoughts.

Scan me

Zodiac and Elements

WATER (Dreamboats) Emotionally fluid and flowing, you are the heart and soul of humanity.

EARTH (Legends) With your feet firmly planted on the ground, you rule the physical world.

FIRE (Stars) Bright, warm and enticing, your love of life is contagious and unstoppable.

AIR (Cool Kids) Fresh as a summer breeze, your cleverness makes the world a better place.

AQUARIUS

Jan 20 – Feb 18

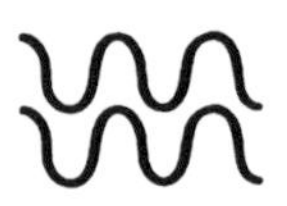

Deep, imaginative, original and unshakable

PISCES

Feb 19 – Mar 20

Affectionate, empathetic, wise and artistic

ARIES

Mar 21 – Apr 19

Eager, dynamic, quick and competitive

TAURUS

Apr 20 – May 20

Strong, dependable, musical and practical

GEMINI

May 21 – Jun 20

Curious, versatile, kind and affectionate

CANCER

Jun 21 – Jul 22

Intuitive, compassionate emotional and protective

LEO

JUL 23 – AUG 22

Dramatic, outgoing, fiery and self-assured

VIRGO

Aug 23 – Sept 22

Organized, loyal, gentle and analytical

LIBRA

Sept 23 – Oct 22

Social, fair-minded, artistic and gracious

SCORPIO

Oct 23 – Nov 21

Passionate, stubborn, resourceful and brave

SAGITTARIUS

Nov 22 – Dec 21

Optimistic, extroverted, funny and generous

CAPRICORN

Dec 22 – Jan 19

Serious, disciplined, hard-working and intelligent

A few fun things about me...

Name

Birthday

Best Feature

Super Power

Good at

Lucky Number

Dog or Cat Person

Favorite Flower

Something weirdly unique about me

ME

MY ZODIAC

LUCKY GEM

I am enough

What self-love looks like

Self-love is one of the most important journeys you'll go on. It takes dedication, practice and can be a little tricky at times... but to live a life that truly makes you happy – it is totally worth it.

Let it gooo!

Letting go of past mistakes

ZZzzzz...

Taking time to rest when you need to

It's OK!

Speaking to yourself with kindness

Not comparing yourself to others

Allowing yourself to do things that you enjoy

Feeling proud of things that you've done well

Let it gooo!

Past mistakes you are ready to let go of:
(Maybe something you said or didn't do)

What did you learn from it?

What do you do during your downtime?

It's OK!

Say something encouraging to yourself:
(Replace self-judgment with self-love)

What do you love the most about yourself that you wish others knew about?

What gives you that warm fuzzy feeling?
(Close your eyes and remember what brings you joy)

Things you are most proud of, big or small:

The story of my life so far....

This is where I am right now.

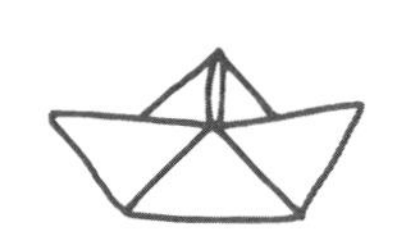

Where I see myself in ten years.

Today I'm super grateful for...

Write or draw all the things - big and small

Do something today that your
future self will thank you for.

I'm not always perfect but I'm always Myself

Decorate each heart with color and
celebrate all your imperfections.
(they need love too!)

It's OK to make mistakes

Perfectionism can be a helpful trait in some situations, but it can also hold you back from taking risks and pursuing your goals. It's okay to make mistakes, because failure is a natural part of the learning process. So let go of the idea of being perfect and instead focus on your progress and self-care.

What task or project have you avoided starting because you fear that you won't complete it perfectly?

What's the worst that could happen if you allow yourself to be less than perfect?

Feel good in 10 minutes

People, things and places that I just adore:

1. One thing that I've worked hard for:

2. Two hobbies or sports I'm passionate about:

3. Three people I can count on for a warm hug and support:

Three things I'm looking forward to:

1

2

3

Positive Self-talk

Words are powerful - just like you!
Write positive sentences for yourself.

I am

I can

I love

I believe

Ask someone who knows you well, what they think you're good at.
(You might be surprised at what they say)

I need to do

More of this...

Less of this...

Write down what your ideal day looks like.
(From when you get up to when you go to sleep)

Write down some things that you've always wanted to try, (even if they scare you a little).

Which one excites you the most?

Find out more about it. (Research through the internet, ask someone who is already doing it...)

Pick a start date:

Weirdest things I've ever...

Eaten

Drunk

Read

Touched

Said

Thought

Seen

Heard

wore

Watched on tv

Written

Some of my favorite things...

BOOK

PERFUME

TV SERIES

MOVIE

FOOD

SNACK

JACAY

MEMORY

CLOTHING

ACCESSORY

Wish list

Want	Need

Today I'm super grateful for...

Write or draw all the things - big and small

Kindness makes you the most
beautiful person in the world,
no matter what you look like.

Stay close to people who feel like Sunshine

Who are the people who feel like sunshine in your life?

What do they do to make you feel so good?

You can not change the people around you, but you can change the people you choose to be around.

Currently happening in my life

LOVING

THINKING

GOING

MAKING

READING

BUYING

EATING

HEARING

WEARING

DOING

Today I'm so grateful for...

Write or draw all the things - big and small

Confidence and intelligence will never stop being beautiful.

Brainstorm your birthday ideas

But you ARE pretty! Pretty kind, pretty smart,
pretty strong and pretty funny.

Birthday Celebration

These are my Birthday plans:

When:

Where:

Who to invite:

What theme / colors:

Decorations:

Birthday Cake:

Party food & drinks:

It isn't about being 'fearless', but how you can 'fear a little less'

What are somethings that you need to fear a little less in your life?

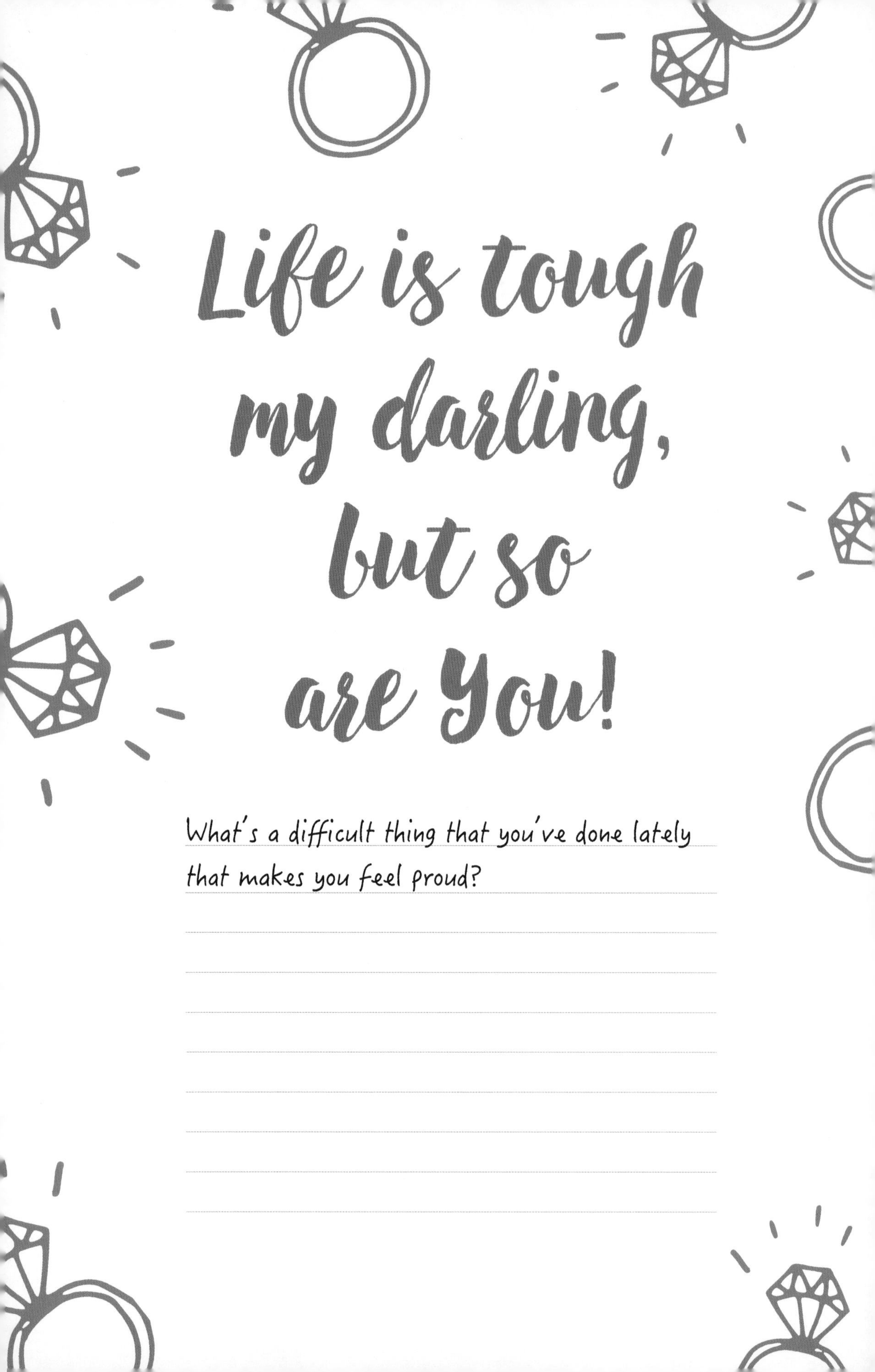

Life is tough my darling, but so are You!

What's a difficult thing that you've done lately that makes you feel proud?

It's OK not to feel happy all the time, but there are simple things you can do to improve your mood when you are feeling blue. Such as...

♥ Pause, reflect and to get to the root of your feelings.

♥ Reach out to a loving, understanding person to talk about how you are feeling.

♥ Cuddle or play with your pet

♥ Listen to uplifting music

♥ Take a twenty minute nap to recharge

♥ Write down your thoughts and feelings

♥ Hug someone

♥ Watch a funny movie...

Can you think of something else to add?

Positive things to do when I feel sad

Draw or write things on this page when you think of them

Kindness is free. Sprinkle that stuff everywhere!

What kind deed have you done lately ?
(no matter how small).

What's something nice you'd like to do for someone?

Your words matter, choose them carefully

Before you speak ask yourself 3 things:

1) Is it true?

2) Is it necessary?

3) Is it kind?

Write down something that you regret saying:

Now give yourself permission to let it go. Letting go of something old makes space for something new!

SPeak
YOUR
TRUTH

Do more of what makes you happy!

I'm most happy when:

My Book list

- ☆☆☆☆☆
- ☆☆☆☆☆
- ☆☆☆☆☆
- ☆☆☆☆☆
- ☆☆☆☆☆
- ☆☆☆☆☆
- ☆☆☆☆☆
- ☆☆☆☆☆
- ☆☆☆☆☆
- ☆☆☆☆☆
- ☆☆☆☆☆
- ☆☆☆☆☆
- ☆☆☆☆☆
- ☆☆☆☆☆
- ☆☆☆☆☆
- ☆☆☆☆☆
- ☆☆☆☆☆
- ☆☆☆☆☆
- ☆☆☆☆☆
- ☆☆☆☆☆

TV Series list

KEY
● Watched ○ Not yet
★★★★★ Amazing
★★★☆☆ Not bad
★☆☆☆☆ Forget it

○ ☆☆☆☆☆
○ ☆☆☆☆☆
○ ☆☆☆☆☆
○ ☆☆☆☆☆
○ ☆☆☆☆☆
○ ☆☆☆☆☆
○ ☆☆☆☆☆
○ ☆☆☆☆☆
○ ☆☆☆☆☆
○ ☆☆☆☆☆
○ ☆☆☆☆☆
○ ☆☆☆☆☆
○ ☆☆☆☆☆
○ ☆☆☆☆☆
○ ☆☆☆☆☆
○ ☆☆☆☆☆
○ ☆☆☆☆☆
○ ☆☆☆☆☆
○ ☆☆☆☆☆
○ ☆☆☆☆☆

My Movie list

KEY
● Watched ○ Not yet
★★★★★ Amazing
★★★☆☆ Not bad
★☆☆☆☆ Forget it

○ ☆☆☆☆☆
○ ☆☆☆☆☆
○ ☆☆☆☆☆
○ ☆☆☆☆☆
○ ☆☆☆☆☆
○ ☆☆☆☆☆
○ ☆☆☆☆☆
○ ☆☆☆☆☆
○ ☆☆☆☆☆
○ ☆☆☆☆☆
○ ☆☆☆☆☆
○ ☆☆☆☆☆
○ ☆☆☆☆☆
○ ☆☆☆☆☆
○ ☆☆☆☆☆
○ ☆☆☆☆☆
○ ☆☆☆☆☆
○ ☆☆☆☆☆
○ ☆☆☆☆☆
○ ☆☆☆☆☆

Brain Dump

THINGS I MUST DO

- [ ]
- [ ]
- [ ]

Nice to do if I have time...

- [ ]
- [ ]
- [ ]

Stop worrying about...

EXPLORE & LEARN

Notes about stuff...

I love who I've been but
I really love who I am becoming...

Success doesn't start in the gym... it starts in your Mind

What does success look like to you?

People said follow your Dreams

☆☆☆☆☆ ♡ ☆☆☆☆☆

...so I went back to bed

What is it that you dream about achieving?(big or small)

How would you feel if your wish came true?

What is it within you that is holding you back?
(which emotion, same old habit)

What do you need to do to overcome these obstacles?
(It's OK to ask for help if you need to)

You don't have to be perfect to be Amazing

There is no one on this planet like you! Embrace and celebrate all the wonderful, quirky and weird things that make up you. Write them down:

Who is someone that you **admire**?
(It could be someone famous or someone you know)

What are the three qualities of this person that you admire?
1)
2)
3)

Awesome! You can only see qualities in someone else that you already have in yourself. Now it's time to find out more about them. If they're famous, read their biography, watch their interviews or if you know them personally interview them yourself.

Be easy on yourself, it takes years to strengthen these qualities but you will get there if you're aware of them and begin to practice them in your daily life.

Remember to breathe

Fill up the space with positive and empowering words

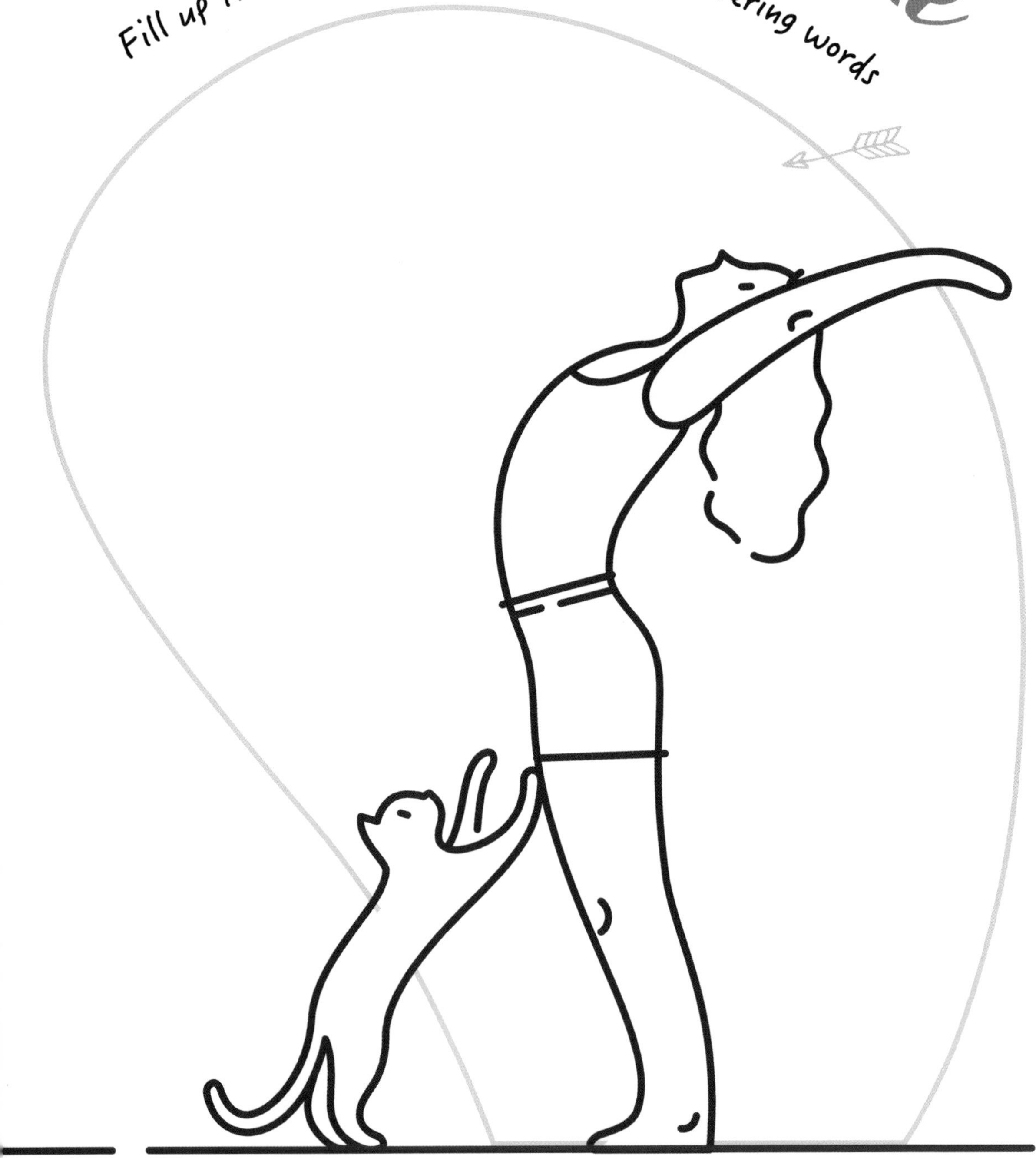

I am becoming more confident & self-loving everyday.

Write an empowering word or positive short message that means something to you on this tee

Brainstorm some ideas:

THANK YOU!
If you've enjoyed this journal
you might like my other books too.
Please visit lizalluma.com
Join LLUMA CLUB for extra goodies
and other fun things - *it's free to join!*
Scan the QR code below or go to:
lizalluma.com/freebies
Scan me

Printed in Great Britain
by Amazon